Time Management

Maximizing Your Achievements By Implementing Efficient Time Management And Enhancing Productivity

(Attain Your Objectives Without Delay, And Enhance Your Efficiency)

Berthold Aschauer

TABLE OF CONTENT

Introduction 1
Strategies For Efficient Time Management Among Students 6
All Eyes Ahead 13
Some Principles 29
The Significance Of A Scheduler 40
10 Lifestyle Habits 49
Establish An Optimal Environment 58
What Steps Or Actions Must One Undertake To Achieve Success? 86
Time Management 89
Strategic Planning Is Crucial: Maintain Comprehensive Lists And Utilize Available Resources 94
"Strategies For Maintaining Singular Focus On Individual Tasks" 108
Block Out Interruptions 128
Creating A System 134

postponement and deferral of responsibilities. As the passage of time ensued, I increasingly perceived the detrimental impact this had on my life. As a consequence, I found myself falling behind in various aspects of my life, including relationships, work obligations, and my overall reputation. Fortunately, I discovered that by enhancing my personal growth and increasing my effectiveness in performing routine tasks, it became significantly easier to exert influence over the positive transformation of my circumstances.

If you have acquired this book, it is evident that you are deeply committed to personal development and possess a genuine determination to assume control over your time and habits. This indicates your desire to enhance yourself and strive for greater accomplishments. Initiating awareness marks the inaugural phase, while steadfastness constitutes a significant portion of the endeavor.

I recommend allocating an ample amount of time to thoroughly engage with the content of this book and contemplate upon the topic highlighted within its pages. Instead of hurrying, feel free to read it twice. I have endeavored to ensure brevity in this book while delivering insightful ideas that facilitate effortless comprehension and assimilation for the reader. I trust that you will derive pleasure from this book, and I assure you that upon its completion, you will possess the resources necessary to effectively manage your time and surmount obstacles in maximizing your daily productivity.

Strategies For Efficient Time Management Among Students

Acquiring the proficiency of effectively managing time is a crucial aptitude that students must perquisite.

However, a significant number of students encounter difficulties in managing their schedules to ensure the timely completion of all their assignments, consequently resulting in heightened levels of stress and frustration.

1) Develop a comprehensive schedule:

Create a comprehensive schedule for your child, enabling them to allocate dedicated time slots for completing their assignments. This will aid in the organization of your child's assignments, allowing them to effectively manage their time and meet deadlines. Utilize distinct colors for each subject to facilitate rapid and effortless comprehension of the schedule by your child.

2) Employ a Schedule:

Assist your child in planning for future assignments by documenting the deadlines in a schedule or planner. Utilize the agenda to allocate dedicated time for television and computer usage as well. By doing so, you can assist your child in circumventing the potential pitfalls of excessive screen time that could detract from their productivity on assignments.

3) Minimize disruptions:

Amidst the prevalence of mobile devices, virtual networking platforms, and interpersonal interactions, students often encounter a multitude of potential diversions that may impede their academic focus. When the moment for getting productive arises, kindly request that your child power off his or her mobile device and log out of all social media profiles. All instances allocated on the master schedule for academic purposes should strictly observe a prohibition on the use of mobile phones and televisions.

4) Establish Objectives for Every Study Session:

Assist your child in establishing precise objectives for each day, such as determining the number of pages to be written for a book report or the quantity of math questions to be solved. The itinerary and comprehensive schedule will facilitate the organization of your child's daily objectives, enabling timely completion of assignments.

5) Commence the preparation of assignments promptly:

Effective time management entails avoiding the procrastination of tasks until the day prior to their deadlines. Allocate a specific time each week to engage in a constructive discussion with your child regarding impending assignments and assessments, thereby facilitating the inclusion of these tasks into their comprehensive timetable and personal planner. Be proactive by allocating a sufficient amount of time ahead of the deadlines to commence the tasks, ensuring your child avoids undue stress and last-minute rush.

6) Establish a Comprehensive Project Plan:

Developing a comprehensive project plan can additionally aid in circumventing the occurrence of eleventh-hour distress. A substantial workload often serves as a prevalent factor contributing to procrastination, thereby resulting in inadequate time management. Assist your child in decomposing assignments into smaller segments, each of which has its own distinct deadlines. This will instigate a sense of foresight in your child, prompting them to initiate tasks well in advance.

7) Focus on a Singular Task at a Time

Although the appearance might suggest increased productivity through multitasking, diverting focus across multiple tasks is not an efficient means of acquiring knowledge. It is imperative that your child focuses their undivided attention on one task at a time. Directing one's attention to a single task will lead to increased efficiency and effectiveness in its completion.

"8) Implement shorter study sessions:

For each half-hour of academic work, it is advisable for your child to allocate a brief intermission of 10-15 minutes in order to rejuvenate. Prolonged focus on a single task can inadvertently trigger students' minds to become more prone to distraction. Incorporating brief intervals of respite provides an effective means to allow your child's cognitive faculties to regenerate, enabling them to return with heightened concentration.

"9) Commence operations at the early hours of the day:

It is advised to instill in your child the habit of commencing their assignments in the early hours of the day, or immediately upon return from school. Please instruct your child to carefully review their agenda and master schedule in order to determine the tasks that must be completed that evening and commence working on them promptly. Postponing the commencement until the later hours of the evening results in a reduced amount of time and energy available to your child, consequently causing their bedtime to be delayed, assignments left incomplete, and ultimately inducing heightened stress for all parties involved.

10) Obtain 8-10 hours of sleep:

It is crucial to ensure that your child obtains sufficient sleep in order to allow their mind to rejuvenate and acquire the necessary energy to remain focused and aligned with their goals the following day. Utilize your comprehensive schedule to designate a specified time each evening for completion of academic tasks, alongside a predetermined hour to retire to bed. Adhering to this established regimen will ensure that your child is afforded ample relaxation time at the conclusion of each day, thus facilitating the attainment of sufficient sleep.

All Eyes Ahead

The maintenance of both your general well-being and your ability to concentrate plays a pivotal role in ensuring your effectiveness and achievements in a professional setting. An effective approach to achieve this objective is by establishing goals and adhering to them. Objectives not only function as markers of progress towards achievement, but they also enhance concentration and focus by offering a defined target to strive for. When we operate with a mere conceptual notion of our objectives, we are restricted to a distant focal point on the horizon as our guiding reference. By establishing checkpoints and objectives to aspire towards, we foster a culture of achievement by enhancing the manageability of tasks and facilitating a heightened concentration on individual components of the entirety.

There exist numerous strategies through which we can incorporate goal-setting behaviors to enhance professional development in the workplace. Goals can be utilized as a strategy to deconstruct substantial tasks into smaller, more manageable components. They can serve as a means to sustain forward progress when engaging in mundane activities. Additionally, goals can facilitate the allocation of concentrated resources towards tasks by subdividing them into smaller, more focused parts. Lastly, goals can serve as a tool to structure our day into efficient and productive segments.

Implement Goal Achieving Apps

In preceding chapters, we have discussed the efficacy of applications in enhancing concentration, focus, and time management competencies within the workplace. Applications can similarly play a substantial role in establishing and attaining objectives within professional settings. By integrating such applications into your professional endeavors, you contribute to enhancing your concentration not just by establishing a roster of tasks to be addressed, but by doing so in a manner that empowers you to pursue incremental objectives, thereby fostering accomplishments.

1. Nozbe is a task management application that offers both free and premium versions. It is specifically developed to enhance efficiency by

facilitating goal setting and the establishment of milestones, ultimately boosting overall performance. If your intention is to wholeheartedly dedicate your efforts towards meticulously executing tasks and affording them the requisite level of consideration, then this application serves as the perfect starting point for you.

2. IRunURun is a mobile application, available in both free and premium versions, that effectively fosters motivation and goal attainment by gamifying the process of setting and achieving targets. Individuals endeavor to achieve an impeccable score of 100 by successfully attaining the objectives they established for the week, yet if these objectives are not met, deductions are made from the score, thereby motivating one to strive for improvement in subsequent attempts.

3. Goals on Track – Goals on track serves as a comprehensive application for both setting and optimizing personal goals related to productivity. Goals on Track, a program that operates on a membership basis, offers a comprehensive graphical representation of goals, the progress made towards them, and the detailed action plans required to facilitate a more nuanced comprehension of effective strategies for achieving those goals.

4. Coach.me provides a convenient solution for managing limited storage space on your mobile device. This complimentary application offers guidance in enhancing productivity, achieving weight loss goals, and improving overall fitness through the implementation of goal-oriented strategies, accompanied by motivational support personnel to propel you towards success.

5. Workshop on Goal Setting: Utilize the Goal & Habit Tracker, a complimentary application that offers comprehensive features for initiating the process of establishing personal and career-related objectives. Engage in a process of ideation to establish objectives, demonstrate dedication to your resolutions, and cultivate the impetus required to realize the goals that you have established by means of this inspiring application.

Common Approaches Employed by Corporations to Attain Objectives

Numerous individuals in the business domain make use of mobile applications to establish, monitor, and accomplish their objectives both in their personal and professional spheres. Furthermore, in conjunction with the utilization of applications, these accomplished individuals effectively employ diverse corporate strategies to attain or amplify these facets of triumph. Let us examine some of the prevailing organizational methodologies employed in attaining goals.

Devote your attention to one objective at a time.

Previously, we have underscored the significance of decomposing tasks into smaller, manageable components. Additionally, we have alluded to the criticality of optimizing concentration to the highest extent achievable. By decomposing tasks into smaller objectives and concentrating on each individual objective separately, you are devoting your complete attention to one constituent element of a final framework and thereby enhancing the overall accuracy of the entire project. By adopting this approach, your attainment of the final goal will be expedited, as it ensures the more effective and expedient completion of your smaller objectives and tasks.

Reassessment

The capacity to temporarily halt and reevaluate objectives is imperative for individuals embarking on any given undertaking. As we advance through the incremental achievements of our objectives, we frequently uncover unanticipated facets, thereby necessitating a reconsideration and modification of both our strategic plans and ultimate aspirations to ensure triumph. Failure to re-evaluate and modify our plans accordingly may result in futile time investment and a failure to reach our ultimate objective.

Utilize the S.M.A.R.T Approach

S.M.A.R.T has been defined as an acronym denoting attributes such as specificity, measurability, achievability, relevance, and time sensitivity. This particular method of goal setting places emphasis on the attainment of goals through the formulation of objectives, employing a set of five criteria.

To achieve success, it is necessary for your goals to be characterized by specificity and the ability to address the questions pertaining to who, what, where, when, which, or why.

Your objectives should also possess measurability. If one is unable to gauge the progress made towards the desired objective and ascertain the ultimate outcomes resulting from its accomplishment, how would one determine the attainment of said objective?

Your objectives must also be reasonable and achievable in order to maintain practicality. Establishing objectives that are beyond reach will only result in inevitable disappointment and squandering of one's time.

Your objectives should possess relevance or hold significance in relation to your business or ongoing project.

It is imperative that your objectives are accompanied by specific timeframes or be subjected to established deadlines.

Through the implementation of this methodology for establishing and accomplishing objectives, you are not only fostering an enhanced comprehension of the task at hand, but you are also paving a trajectory towards the attainment of your ultimate goal.

Reference Locke and Latham

Locke and Latham have gained recognition for their formulation of the five principles of goal setting, which delineate the process of establishing explicit and achievable objectives. The approach advocated by Locke and Latham places significant emphasis on the principles of Clarity, Challenge, Commitment, Feedback, and Task Complexity.

To be attainable, a goal must be clearly articulated. Establishing precise objectives enables individuals to discern their exact aspirations, thus allowing them to channel their attention and efforts towards their realization.

In order to achieve success, it is imperative that goals possess an element of difficulty. The establishment of ambitious objectives serves as a catalyst for our determination to endeavor towards their attainment, while the establishment of attainable objectives demands less effort on our part.

For a goal to be effectively achieved, it is imperative that we demonstrate unwavering commitment towards it. If we establish a goal devoid of our dedication, our motivation to achieve such a goal diminishes. Rather, establish objectives that you can wholeheartedly dedicate yourself to; objectives that hold personal significance for various reasons.

To achieve our objectives, it is essential to actively pursue counsel and constructive input. To ensure an accurate assessment of our progress towards a goal, it is imperative to actively solicit feedback and guidance from individuals who can provide insights on any potential deviations from our initial trajectory. Receiving advice and feedback serves as a valuable means to evaluate the possibility of unproductive efforts and time wastage.

Finally, for goals to be attainable, they should not possess excessive complexity. If one encounters a task of significant complexity, it might be prudent to analyze the opportunity of subdividing it into more manageable objectives or exploring alternative approaches to accomplish it. When individuals formulate goals of excessive complexity, they frequently subject themselves to an overwhelming burden, consequently resulting in burnout and diminished focus.

Engage in the process of defining goals and measuring outcomes.

A highly straightforward strategy for goal setting and accomplishment involves the establishment of objectives and the identification of the anticipated outcomes, commonly referred to as key results. In order for goals to be efficacious, it is essential to establish the purpose or aim of said goals - what exact outcome are we endeavoring to achieve? What is the ultimate outcome we aim to achieve through our development efforts? After defining our goals, we need to examine the pivotal outcomes we strive to achieve. These key outcomes are derived from the underlying goals. As an illustration, our aim in establishing a goal could be to foster a more efficient framework within our Human Resources department. The anticipated outcome of this objective is a 50% enhancement in communication between the general workforce and the HR department.

The primary objective of establishing OKRs is to delineate objectives, elucidate their purposes, and construct a streamlined framework illustrating how goals can be effectively leveraged to attain success.

Some Principles

These principles have the potential to positively transform your life, provided that you diligently engage with the provided information and effectively implement them. I strongly uphold the belief that knowledge devoid of action holds no value. Carefully peruse and repeatedly review each principle until you have attained a thorough comprehension of their significance and the profound effects that implementing them can have on your existence. If you desire to achieve greater productivity within the allotted time, implementing these 8 principles guarantees the desired outcome.

Please pause and make a solemn pledge to imbue your life with at least one, if not all, of these 8 principles. This commitment must not be regarded frivolously. You have acquired this book with the intention of witnessing tangible outcomes, and I assure you that if you wholeheartedly dedicate yourself to the principles outlined herein and exert diligent effort, you shall experience a profound and enduring transformation in your life.

Initiate Your Day on a Positive Note

Individuals who achieve success adhere to a structured regimen. They arise at designated moments and initiate their day in a manner conducive to achieving utmost productivity. Individuals who achieve success possess a comprehension of the significance of optimal nourishment and methods to stimulate their cognitive and physical faculties. Tony Robbins, a well-regarded speaker and esteemed life coach, imparts wisdom through a practice known as the "hour of power".

The purpose behind this hour of power is to arise from rest and engage in physical activity. This does not imply that you must rise and engage in running a marathon, but it does indicate that when your alarm sounds, you ought to get out of bed. Please refrain from pressing the snooze button, abstain from checking your emails on your phone, resist the urge to browse Facebook, and instead, promptly rise and engage in physical activity.

I have discovered that by placing my alarm clock at a distance from my bed, I have been able to compel myself to rise even in instances where I lacked the desire to do so. I maintain a hydration routine by placing a filled sports bottle adjacent to my bedside alarm clock, and promptly consume its contents upon awakening. This practice facilitates the initiation of your metabolism while simultaneously replenishing the hydration levels within your cells. The subsequent step in my regimen involves engaging in stretching and physical fitness activities. Developing and maintaining physical fitness will provide you with increased vitality, vigor, and a profound sense of achievement.

The following outlines how one ought to allocate the initial hour of their day. By failing to prioritize self-care and hastily preparing for work after oversleeping, you are essentially disregarding your personal well-being and impeding your progress towards accomplishing your objectives. It would be advisable for you to consider retiring to bed earlier or sacrificing a portion of your sleep in order to commence this morning routine. I understand that you may be questioning whether it is recommended to obtain a minimum of 8 hours of sleep per night. This topic has generated considerable debate, with scientists yet to ascertain a definitive rationale for the necessity of sleep. The detrimental consequences and profound outcomes of prolonged sleep deprivation are readily observable, yet the underlying causes remain elusive. I recall having perused material indicating that President Trump's sleep patterns consist of a mere 5-6 hours per night. Additionally, anecdotal accounts have suggested that both Einstein and Edison adopted a strategy of "catnapping" rather than adhering to traditional sustained nocturnal slumber. I am not suggesting that you cease your sleep, but rather proposing that the advantages you will accrue by rising an hour earlier to commence your morning with purpose will surpass the hour of sleep you may forego.

~ DEVISE A STRATEGY AND EXECUTE IT ~

This is an essential aspect of effective time management and crucial for achieving the desired outcomes. Consider it from this perspective... In what manner do you plan on achieving outcomes when you possess a lack of certainty regarding your intended objectives? Establishing a coherent set of objectives will provide not only purpose to your life but also a sense of fulfillment as you strive towards their attainment.

The majority of individuals fail to comprehend the significance of effectively managing their time, or to acknowledge the value of documenting each task by either writing it down on paper or typing and printing it out. It is highly convenient for an individual to express their intention to undertake

____ without manifesting any tangible progress towards its achievement. When one transcribes their tasks onto paper, they are establishing an informal commitment, and this act of documenting facilitates deeper contemplation and consideration for each task.

When delineating your daily agenda, it is crucial to allocate additional contemplation towards it. I employ the structure; Pardon me? Why? How? I have discovered that I possess the capability to consistently produce and accomplish to-do lists. The "What?" refers to the task at hand, and occasionally, we may fail to articulate it in a manner that accurately reflects the necessary actions. Consequently, this may lead to subsequent modifications. The inquiry behind your motivation to accomplish that task lies in the essence of "Why?" Determining the underlying motivation behind your desire to achieve this objective will lend it greater significance and direction. The "How?" section entails a comprehensive compilation where you document various methodologies that can potentially be employed to successfully complete the assigned undertaking. Occasionally, there exist various approaches to tackling a problem, and documenting them will provide you with a more comprehensive perspective on the optimal strategy for achieving the task at hand.

Example

Achieve a weight reduction of 10lbs within a span of 90 days

In order to enhance my energy levels and bolster my self-assurance. Improving my physical fitness will enhance my self-esteem and contribute to an extended, more prosperous, and contented existence.

How - Modify my dietary regimen, engage in physical exercise thrice weekly at a fitness facility, incorporate running into my routine, partake in swimming sessions multiple times per week, become a member of a fitness collective, endeavor to achieve a daily step count of at least 10,000, refrain from dining at external establishments during lunchtime, proactively prepare my meals for the forthcoming week, and so forth...

The significance of employing this approach while formulating your daily agenda lies in the fact that it establishes a compelling incentive to fulfill your tasks and may potentially underscore the dissatisfaction that failing to achieve desired outcomes will entail. As you may observe, I have enumerated several distinct methods for attaining my desired weight loss of 10 pounds. Once you have formulated your inventory of strategies for achieving your goals, you can proceed to condense that compilation into a selection of the three or four primary approaches you aspire to integrate into your daily routine.

By documenting these supplementary ideas, you have now established a series of contingency plans. These contingency plans prove useful in the event that circumstances prevent you from continuing an activity relied upon to accomplish your objective. For example, suppose you made the decision to pursue running but subsequently experienced a knee injury. Swimming was included among the items listed under the category of "How?". Swimming is a low-impact exercise that carries no risk of aggravating the injury, while still yielding favorable outcomes.

The Significance Of A Scheduler

When embarking on a journey to an unfamiliar nation or metropolis, one may find oneself unacquainted with the local thoroughfares. It presents a novel environment for you—where each encounter with different parts of the city brings uncertainty. Now, would you be able to conceive of traveling to this unfamiliar nation devoid of a smartphone? I am confident that you would experience a sense of alarm, similar to my own. What is the cause for manifesting distress in the event that we neglect to carry our smartphones? In addition to the acknowledged rationale behind our smartphone dependency, we rely on Google Maps as a means of navigating unfamiliar urban environments. Maps provide a visual representation of anticipated scenarios and navigational directions. We utilize the provided information in order to maneuver within the urban landscape and achieve our intended objective. Likewise, in the pursuit of myriad objectives in our existence, it becomes imperative to seek an authoritative reference, a parallel navigational aid that delineates our path on a daily basis, steering us through our expedition towards the ultimate destination. The importance of possessing a productivity planner is highlighted in this chapter, as it serves as a means of assistance in such situations.

Consider this chapter as the inception of your journey. Prior to embarking on our expedition, it is imperative that we adequately prepare ourselves and gather the necessary items. The incorporation of a planner serves as an excellent initial step towards effectively executing your pursuit of heightened productivity. I cannot overemphasize the profound impact this habit has had on my life. I previously identified as an individual lacking direction and purpose. I frequently found myself devoid of knowledge in the majority of situations due to my inclination to retain all information solely within my mental faculties. Previously, I held the belief that I was devoid of any sense of purpose or had exhausted my well of innovative ideas. Nevertheless, that was not the primary cause. This is due to the fact that I have failed to render my thoughts into written form. The human mind serves as a profoundly captivating realm to ignite imaginativeness, yet it also proves to be a challenging domain for sustaining those ideas. The majority of individuals will encounter difficulty in maintaining a concept or task within our cognitive faculties for a sufficient duration to fully retain and mentally organize them. Consequently, I commenced by documenting my goals, ideas, and tasks on a sheet of A4 paper. As a result, I proceeded to compose content on numerous additional A4 sheets, ultimately acquiring a dedicated planner - a literary artifact in which all my plans and goals were diligently inscribed, providing me with the necessary direction and stimulus to accomplish tasks.

Through consistent use of my planner, it became apparent to me that I was not an individual lacking a plan or purpose. I possessed numerous responsibilities and aspirations to fulfill throughout my existence on this celestial body. I failed to comprehend this situation as I retained all information internally and solely indulged in fantasies about it. When I committed those thoughts to writing, they underwent a transition phase. At that point in time, my sole focus and utmost concern revolved around achieving what I had put into writing. And you will come to the same realization regarding yourself once you initiate the practice of organizing your tasks and appointments in a planner. Please refrain from regarding your planner as solely a tool for organizing your daily tasks or assisting in tidying up any disorder. Consider this as a unique chance to further explore your innermost self and devise strategies to enhance your personal growth and refinement.

The Advantages of Utilizing a Scheduler

Utilizing a scheduler in close proximity and entering relevant details can enhance your ability to maintain a high level of organization. I will expound upon several rationales as to why incorporating a planner is an imperative tool to employ when embarking upon your journey towards enhanced productivity. Once you have comprehended the underlying rationale, we can proceed to examine methodologies by which you can employ it to facilitate efficient strategic planning.

Prioritizes Important Activities

In essence, a planner facilitates the distinction of one's fundamental objectives. You are afforded the liberty to document any engagements within a scheduling tool. Every piece of written content is automatically stored and subsequently printed onto a physical sheet of paper. A planner aids in the arrangement and management of your engagements, enabling you to effectively prioritize and complete the most essential and pressing tasks. Think about it. We have a multitude of tasks to attend to when our schedules become occupied. However, one's busy schedule does not imply engagement in unproductive endeavors. Upon transcribing these activities onto your planner, you will have the opportunity to reconsider them and remove any unproductive endeavors. Furthermore, you may choose to prioritize endeavors that contribute to your personal growth and the betterment of both yourself and your immediate environment. We will provide a comprehensive discussion on the topic of priorities in Chapter 4.

A Reliable Reminder

As previously stated, the human brain serves as a suboptimal repository for preserving concepts. Consider ideas as a highly unstable compound when it resides in our cognitive faculties. It has the potential to rapidly dissipate in a matter of seconds if no proactive measures are implemented. Therefore, upon the translation of these concepts and strategies into a planner, the resultant outcome is one that is stable and resistant to change. Each time you access your planner and peruse its contents, it serves as a prompt for your pending tasks and responsibilities. It is a commendable approach to remain focused and accomplish the intended tasks. You will never forgo any engagements due to cognitive lapses, as your planner has transformed into a dependable companion, faithfully prompting you of your intentions.

A Time Manager

The primary objective of this book is to assist you in effectively managing your time. That is the core role of a planner. When employing a planner, one shall apportion designated time intervals for their daily activities. Having a clear understanding of your scheduled tasks and obligations for specific times and days in a given week promotes effective task management and facilitates their successful completion. Additionally, after accomplishing the MITs (Most Important Tasks) of the day, it affords you the opportunity to indulge in other activities of a creative and enjoyable nature. Therefore, your scheduler serves as a proficient time management tool, enabling you to strategically plan and assign time intervals for the efficient management of all your responsibilities.

10 Lifestyle Habits

One's health status and level of energy in approaching life are determined by their lifestyle patterns. If you make it a point to address any of these habits that you have been neglecting, it will significantly alter the overall situation.

Prioritize an adequate amount of rest – This is of paramount importance as sleep serves as a crucial period for the body to repair itself and regulate the release of hormones that aid in the healing process. These techniques also enhance your psychological perspective and approach to life. It is imperative to ensure that you obtain a full 8 hours of undisturbed sleep each night in order to optimize cognitive function the subsequent day.

Consume nutritious food - This necessitates eliminating all unhealthy choices. Consume a substantial amount of fresh food in lieu of indulging excessively in carbohydrate-rich options. The issue with contemporary lifestyle lies in its promotion of snacking, which consistently leads to detrimental health outcomes. Take a break for a midday meal, in order to replenish your energy levels for the remainder of the afternoon.

Engage in adequate physical activity - Physical exercise is essential for generating energy. That is the functioning mechanism of the human body. The endorphins released during physical activity elicit a profound sense of well-being, which can transform the perception of exercise from aversion to enjoyable engagement. Engage in activities that bring you true pleasure while simultaneously engaging in physical exercise.

The subsequent four habits necessitate some effort on your part, as they assist you in establishing essential life routines and identifying your aspirations. If one lacks a clear understanding of their objectives, how can they aspire to achieve great heights? The issue lies in the fact that individuals tend to fall short of their maximum capabilities in the absence of a well-defined strategy. Accordingly, these practices center on formulating a strategy and adhering to it:

Record, or compile, a schedule of your tasks for tomorrow - These goals should initially be set as attainable goals, as your mind is not yet accustomed to adhering to a structured plan. Subsequently, one should elevate the objectives to encompass weekly and potentially monthly benchmarks.

Develop a life strategy - Undoubtedly, this strategy may evolve with the passing of time, nevertheless, contemplate your aspirations and objectives for your life trajectory. Please attempt to chart or outline it. The issue individuals face resides in their tendency to disregard the future due to perceiving it as too distant and unimportant to address. By formulating a concrete strategy, one inherently permits the harmonization of their immediate objectives within the overarching framework. For example, when Alice aspired to establish a flower shop, she possessed a definitive objective. Despite lacking the necessary funds, her actions exhibited great prudence and thoughtfulness. She pursued her dream step by step, starting with employment at a florist shop, where she diligently acquired skills in the profession, honed her abilities in handling both vendors and customers, and diligently accumulated savings to advance towards her ultimate objective. If a strategic blueprint is absent, endeavor to envision the trajectory you aspire to embark upon in your life, ensuring a high level of precision and clarity. Having well-defined objectives enhances your ability to achieve greater accomplishments in your life.

Recreation and satisfaction - It is imperative to maintain equilibrium in one's life, ensuring that neither work nor personal commitments overshadow the other. Achieving equilibrium stems from establishing a schedule that harmoniously accommodates both aspects of your life, allowing you to dedicate your utmost efforts to both personal connections and your professional pursuits. Strive to cultivate a consistent practice of establishing appropriate boundaries to avoid any encroachment or overlap. Building and nurturing relationships require a significant investment of time and effort. Work requires commitment. Neither should take precedence. Consequently, if one must adapt their objectives to align harmoniously with both professional obligations and personal life, such adjustments should be embraced.

Try to avoid excesses. Excessive consumption of cigarettes can be fatal. Excessive consumption of alcohol will have similar implications. If you can adapt your conduct in such a manner as to avoid extremes, you can derive pleasure from both pursuits while mitigating potential risks. There is a wide array of options readily accessible in the present era. One might inquire as to the relevance of this matter to your work methods and productivity. It affects it. If you need to repeatedly exit the premises for a smoking break, it considerably hampers the efficiency and pace of your work. Excessive consumption of alcohol necessitates a period of recovery in order to regain productivity. Consider it from this perspective - exercising restraint in all matters.

Associate with individuals who foster a positive sense of self, as doing so can greatly enhance your productivity by ensuring their feedback is consistently uplifting and affirming. Minimizing your interactions with individuals who discourage or hinder your progress enables you to maintain a sense of confidence and effectively manage your emotions, ultimately preserving your focus on tasks at hand.

Ensure punctuality - If you are among those who constantly experience apprehension regarding appointments, adopt an alternative approach. Commence your journey earlier and arrive punctually. It is consistent across all domains of your existence. You garner increased admiration for maintaining punctuality, an attribute that will propel you towards elevated levels of achievement and efficiency.

Develop the skill of attentive receptiveness - By being receptive, individuals acquire a greater breadth of knowledge. When one is excessively preoccupied with expressing personal viewpoints, one may overlook significant information. Please endeavor to maintain silence and strive to hone your active listening skills, as doing so will unveil numerous opportunities for you.

These are all lifestyle choices or habits that ought to already be integrated into your daily routine. I dare say that some of these habits are ones you have inadvertently overlooked over a duration of time. Get them back. They possess immense value and will significantly enhance your productivity and empower you to accomplish more in your life. If you happen to struggle with any of these lifestyle habits, make a concerted effort to improve in that area. Identify your strengths and duly acknowledge them, then proceed to address areas that you are aware of being your personal weaknesses.

Establish An Optimal Environment

Regardless of whether you are working remotely or in a traditional workplace setting, the surrounding environment holds utmost significance Engaging in work from the comfort of your own residence may present certain challenges. You need not be concerned with commuting and are at liberty to dress as you please, although it necessitates a greater level of commitment and self-drive. However, my intention is not to promote the concept of remote work. I would like to engage in a discussion regarding the surrounding conditions of your surroundings.

Many individuals hold the belief that productivity is commonly disrupted by significant factors, whereas in reality, it is the minor occurrences that transpire throughout the day that largely affect it.

The primary determinant in this case is the surrounding environment.

Minor tasks such as locating a charger may require only a few seconds or a minute to complete, yet they disrupt your productive state for a considerable period of thirty minutes or longer. You desire the workspace to be productive and stimulating.

If the environment in which you operate fails to elicit inspiration and motivation, it will prove exceedingly difficult to accomplish any tasks.

Productive Office Space

Organizations desire enhanced productivity among their workforce; however, discerning the exact manifestation of such productivity within an office environment remains a pertinent question. Achieving high levels of productivity is not synonymous with rapid completion of tasks or reaching a destination swiftly. Rather, it pertains to reaching the destination with utmost efficiency while maintaining one's mental well-being. The significance of a person's individual workspace often goes unnoticed when it comes to productivity. Regardless of whether you rummage through the drawers in search of a document or your desk is cluttered with an excess of trinkets, establishing an organized and optimal desk arrangement is crucial for achieving success.

Facilitate an opportunity for mobility.

A highly effective approach to maintaining concentration involves recognizing the moment when one encounters a barrier to productivity. Upon doing so, engaging in a brief stroll may assist in attaining a fresh outlook. Furthermore, extensive research supports this claim. Numerous investigations have demonstrated that incorporating intervals of cognitive relaxation within one's workday can significantly enhance productivity. Engaging in brief strolls throughout the day can effectively mitigate stress levels and enhance overall well-being.

The inclusion of an adjustable desk that facilitates both sitting and standing positions can prove beneficial, and it is common for numerous workplaces to permit the use of such furnishings. There are alternative activities that you can engage in to facilitate motion. Placing the phone and copy machine in a separate room or at a considerable distance, along with establishing a centralized area for accessing water, coffee, and other refreshments, will provide individuals with an incentive to engage in physical movement.

Incorporate a botanical element onto your workspace.

Occasionally, implementing a minor alteration can greatly enhance your level of productivity, for instance, by maintaining a small botanical specimen within your office premises or on your workspace. This contributes to creating a vibrant atmosphere in your living area. Houseplants can be highly advantageous in enhancing productivity. In 2014, a research team in the United Kingdom made a notable discovery indicating that the presence of plants in the work environment was associated with a noteworthy increase in productivity, amounting to a 15 percent improvement. Moreover, this study found that the inclusion of plants also enhanced overall workplace satisfaction and fostered higher levels of work engagement.

Provide a designated space for your electronic devices.

Tablets, smartphones, and similar electronic devices have the potential to enhance organization and productivity.

However, they can also be considered an effective means of squandering one's time. Research has revealed the detrimental impact of smartphones on one's level of productivity. According to a conducted survey, it was revealed that employees allocated a total of five hours per week engaging in non-work-related activities on their mobile devices.

One effective method to circumvent this diversion is to locate a designated area to store your electronic devices during your work periods. This could serve as a compartment that you can empty to specifically accommodate and store your electronic devices. In the event that you are unable to visually perceive them, you will consequently refrain from succumbing to the temptation of utilizing them.

Ensure that your space is cleaned on a daily basis.

Maintaining an organized work environment can enhance levels of productivity. Discard unnecessary items and ensure the proper maintenance of your organizational system to minimize unnecessary diversions. The presence of a disorganized work environment will give rise to a greater number of challenges compared to generating innovative concepts. According to research, a considerable number of employees dedicate approximately thirty-eight hours per annum to the task of locating misplaced or lost items. That equates to nearly a full workweek.

In addition to daily maintenance and tidying, allocate a portion of your day's conclusion to meticulously structure your agenda, thereby ensuring clear prioritization for the subsequent day.

Exercise discretion when adding personal touches to your designated area.

Enhancing the ambience of your office environment with personalized elements can foster a stronger emotional engagement with your work. However, exercise caution to avoid excessive embellishments that may lead to clutter. Strive to achieve equilibrium between items that hold significance and those that offer practical utility. A desktop calendar could prove to be beneficial. Furthermore, it is possible to incorporate an image portraying an individual or object that elicits inspiration within you.

Ensure your personal comfort.

In an ideal scenario, you would have the ability to regulate the temperature within your designated area to achieve an optimal level of comfort. Regrettably, for individuals employed within office premises, this option is unfeasible. However, alternative measures can be employed. Initially, endeavor to inquire about the possibility of requesting an adjustment to the thermostat in order to increase the temperature. A study conducted by Cornell University has revealed that temperatures below 68 degrees Fahrenheit have the potential to lead to an increased occurrence of errors and a consequent decline in productivity. Conversely, temperatures exceeding 68 degrees Fahrenheit have the potential to enhance productivity. Please ensure you have a jacket or sweater readily available in your office to address any potential temperature-related discomfort that may arise.

Make a suitable music selection or opt for silence.

For numerous individuals, the most effective approach to immerse themselves in their work entails wearing noise-canceling headphones and playing music at high volume. Numerous studies have demonstrated the efficacy of this approach. Determining the optimal music selection can present challenges, yet employing platforms such as Pandora or Spotify can enhance the process due to their provision of productivity-oriented playlists.

If music proves to be ineffective, then that is acceptable. Indeed, certain scholarly investigations have put forth the claim that music may pose as a source of distraction. If you experience difficulty in maintaining focus in the presence of music, it is advisable to embrace the absence of sound.

Please incorporate items of a yellow hue. The majority of office buildings are adorned with somber grays and neutral hues. Although this color scheme is devoid of any distracting elements, it fails to effectively stimulate individuals in any manner. According to the principles of color theory, red is regarded as the most invigorating.

Nevertheless, the color red is associated with numerous negative connotations, such as rage. Yellow is considered to be among the most effective hues for enhancing one's workspace and cultivating a more invigorating environment. It provides an equivalent level of productivity as red, while being devoid of any adverse consequences.

Desk Space

We have briefly discussed the contents of your desk, but now let us delve into the optimal organization of your workspace to ensure maximum productivity and minimize potential distractions. All the topics under consideration are universally applicable, encompassing individuals engaged in remote work as well as those employed within conventional office premises.

You will dedicate approximately 50 percent of your workday to beholding the contents of your desk; hence, it is prudent to ensure that it is equipped with items that inspire and enhance your productivity.

Plants

As previously mentioned, and reiterated presently, the inclusion of a plant complements the ambience of your environment by infusing it with a sense of vitality. You do not need to possess an authentic botanical specimen. An artificial plant is also an option you can consider.

Candles

In certain office buildings, the use of lighted candles may not be permitted. However, it is not necessary to even ignite them. Candles, particularly those imbued with fragrance, contribute to a state of relaxation and inner tranquility. This can facilitate the generation and development of your ideas. The presence of candles lends an air of elegance to your desk.

Motivational quotations or prints

If you possess a wall, proceed to affix these upon it. Although it may seem cliché, surrounding oneself with inspirational quotes or artistic prints can be an effective means of fostering motivation and overcoming a state of inertia.

Photographs displayed within frames

Framed photographs are likely to be among the initial items individuals incorporate into their desk settings. You have the opportunity to populate the frame with family members, pets, or any other source of inspiration and motivation that encourages your ongoing efforts.

Vibrantly-hued writing utensils

It is advisable to keep writing instruments readily accessible, as one cannot predict when the need to jot something down might arise. It is enjoyable to possess pens of diverse colors.

Utilizing weekly organizers and adhesive notes

Post-it notes are an optimal resource for promptly recording brief ideas and messages. Weekly planners assist in maintaining organization or have the capacity to create the perception of organization in one's mind. Additionally, you have the option to add vibrant colors to enhance the ambiance of your workspace.

Noticeboards

Noticeboards are exceptionally beneficial due to their capacity for accommodating multiple items of interest. To these notebooks, one can append a variety of items such as task lists, schedules, annotated post-it's, images, captivating memes, and prompts, among other possibilities.

Additionally, these items are also available in a variety of colors.

Enhance the appearance of your computer

Given that you spend a significant amount of your day in its presence, wouldn't it be worthwhile to enhance its aesthetic appeal? Acquire a protective laptop case and personalized decal. This method provides an excellent means of differentiating your computer from others'. Furthermore, it enhances the ambiance of your office environment. The utilization of a keyboard decal can effectively serve the purpose of safeguarding your computer against dust particles and other potential hazards that may come into contact with the keys. Additionally, it has the capability to evoke the sensation of possessing a freshly acquired computer.

Lamp

Possessing a desk lamp is advantageous if one intends to engage in nocturnal work. Nobody desires to work past regular working hours, but occasionally, it becomes necessary, and on certain occasions, that is precisely when creative ideas strike. It is imperative to possess a lamp for one's work in the dimly-lit winter months and during the nocturnal hours. No one desires to experience a headache as a result of inadequate lighting.

Snacks

The act of pausing to obtain nourishment can cause recurrent disruptions to individuals on multiple occasions throughout the day. Equipping your workspace with readily accessible snacks, such as nuts or fruits, is highly advisable. In this manner, you will not be required to rise from your position should you experience slight hunger. Additionally, it is advisable to have one or two water bottles conveniently located in your vicinity.

Trashcan

There are two rationales for the presence of a waste receptacle in close proximity. Initially, it will prevent your desk from becoming cluttered, thus enabling you to maintain an organized workspace. Additionally, it will enhance your efficiency by eliminating the need to interrupt your work in order to relocate to a different location for the purpose of disposing waste.

Calendar

Calendars signify one's propensity for organization, which in turn leads to heightened productivity. The presence of a calendar within immediate reach will facilitate visualizing your scheduled events for the duration of the month. By utilizing this method, there is no need for you to engage in the process of searching through your mobile device or computer to locate your schedule, as it will be readily accessible to you.

Home Office

Although the aforementioned rules encompass the general guidelines for any given environment, certain additional rules can be observed when organizing a home office setting. As aforementioned, operating from one's residence necessitates a higher degree of determination and concentration. Hence, it is crucial that the surroundings are conducive to productivity rather than hindering it.

Incorporate a soothing aroma into your living space.

This may not be achievable in a traditional office setting, but it can be accomplished within the confines of a personal home office. The utilization of fragranced candles, incense, or essential oils such as jasmine and lavender can be advantageous in providing natural enhancements to cognitive function. Aromatherapy may be the solution that can assist you in regaining your focus and achieving your goals.

Please identify a suitable area within your dwelling that caters to your needs.

This has the potential to encompass an entirely distinct chamber or a designated segment within the existing space. Please make a determination regarding the orientation of your desk, either facing the wall or positioned by a window. Determine the most suitable space for your needs. Every individual possesses unique qualities. Certain individuals find that working at their kitchen table is conducive to their productivity. Certain individuals may opt to conduct their work activities within the confines of their bedrooms, while others may choose to utilize their living room coffee tables for such purposes. If, indeed, you possess a distinct chamber in which to establish your domestic work environment, you have the opportunity to craft a personal sanctuary that fosters integrity and creativity, thereby aiding your steadfastness towards your professional objectives. If it is the case that you are limited to utilizing merely a portion of an existing room, there is no cause for concern; rest assured, you still have the capacity to fashion an outstanding office area.

Position yourself in proximity to an electrical socket.

In the present day, it is commonplace for individuals to possess mobile devices such as smartphones and laptops. If one is engaged in professional pursuits, it is imperative to possess a laptop for the purpose of carrying out work-related tasks. Our operational capability is contingent upon maintaining a sufficient level of battery charge. Ensure that your laptop and phone remain consistently charged by positioning your workspace in close proximity to an electrical socket. Should you be unable to accomplish that, I would advise considering the acquisition of an extension cord as a means of ensuring that you are never impeded by a low battery.

Ensure that your office space is adequately illuminated.

Working in dim lighting may exert strain on your eyes, which is not desirable. Ensure that your home office is adequately illuminated, ideally through the inclusion of natural light. Following the consumption of a cup of coffee in the morning, exposure to natural light will aid in awakening oneself each day. Furthermore, it may be advantageous to acquire a desk lamp, as the availability of optimal sunlight through the window cannot be guaranteed at all times.

Incorporate elements that personally inspire and motivate individuals.

One of the advantageous aspects of remote work is the freedom to personalize and adorn your office and workspace to your own preferences. If you desire to adorn your wall with photographs depicting your family during their vacation, feel free to proceed. Would photographs showcasing prospective holiday destinations serve as a source of encouragement for you? Please also proceed with suspending them. Incorporating verdant flora can further enhance the ambiance and offer a source of revitalizing oxygen. If you experience allergic reactions to plants, it would be advisable to select an alternative option. Perhaps you have an affinity for candles or prefer a minimalist aesthetic, whichever aligns with your preference, include it in your space. The primary objective is to refrain from incorporating elements that will consistently captivate your focus and divert you from your intended tasks.

Please refrain from having any televisions within your office premises.

Indeed, televisions can greatly contribute to relaxation or serve as pleasant ambient noise during household chores. However, they fall short of being conducive to building a highly productive work atmosphere. Being in close proximity to your living room, where the sound of the TV can be audible, has the potential to cause significant distractions, particularly when you are aware that your favorite show is being broadcasted. The television has a strong ability to captivate and engross individuals. They serve as a convenient means to relax after enduring a prolonged period of activity, yet it is imperative to refrain from indulging in them during your designated working hours. Nevertheless, should you exhibit self-restraint for a duration of only thirty minutes to an hour, you may partake in television viewing during your midday reprieve, thereby availing oneself of yet another advantage of remote work.

Please ensure that you are able to maintain a state of comfort.

Throughout the day, it is highly probable that you will be predominantly seated, hence it is imperative to ensure that your seating arrangement is designed for comfort. While we are engaged in these tasks, it would be advantageous for you to enhance productivity while ensuring your physical comfort. If necessary, adjust your laptop position to align with eye level. Employing remote work arrangements can offer a multitude of advantages that contribute to heightened levels of comfort and convenience. There is no need for you to lend an ear to individuals who express dissatisfaction about the air conditioning or experience the chilling gusts of winter entering through an open window due to someone feeling excessively warm.

Additionally, it would be beneficial to engage in desk exercises and take periodic walks in order to prevent prolonged periods of slouching in front of your computer throughout the day. It can be observed that certain workplaces promote the utilization of standing desks in order to align computer screens with the level of the eyes. You have the option to either acquire a standing desk for experimentation or invest in a fresh cushion for your chair—select the alternative that brings you comfort.

Minimize the number of distractions to the best of your ability.

The efficacy of your workspace can be determined by the level of productivity you are able to achieve. Experiment with various areas within your residence to ascertain the most suitable one for your needs. Though the act of indulging in the view of your garden on a daily basis may possess an air of romance, it might result in a diversion of your attention from productive endeavors, leading to a decrease in actual work accomplished. If you happen to keep animals outdoors, it might not be advisable to position yourself within view of their activities, as this may lead to prolonged distraction from observing their playful behavior throughout the day.

Seek out a secluded area where you can enjoy uninterrupted tranquility. Please ensure to communicate to your family members that they are kindly requested not to disturb you while you are occupying your office area and engaging in work tasks. Regardless of whether or not this implies a restriction on their entry into your home office or bedroom until six, it is imperative to ensure that they comprehend your unavailability to engage in conversation or play due to your remote work commitments. If your mobile device proves to be a source of constant distraction, and its usage is not intrinsic to your professional obligations, it is advisable to relocate it elsewhere. One will be astounded by the noticeable improvement in productivity when the absence of telephones within the office environment is ensured.

Please adhere to a professional dress code as if you were in a formal work setting.

Although this statement may not be well-received by individuals who work from home, it is worth mentioning that wearing pajamas may not be the most conducive attire for optimal productivity. It is advisable to attire yourself in the morning prior to commencing your day in order to avoid unexpected rushes and distress when confronted with the need to appear presentable for a video conference or outings. Furthermore, the act of presenting oneself in appropriate attire can enhance one's sense of professionalism and effectively approach tasks with greater efficiency.

What Steps Or Actions Must One Undertake To Achieve Success?

Attaining long-term success for your personal and professional aspirations culminates in the accomplishment of executing twice the workload within half the duration.
Prior to enhancing your productivity, it is imperative to heighten your level of concentration and attentiveness by eliminating any superfluous endeavors that are unrelated to your objectives, such as activities that consume time or result in distraction.

Initially, it is imperative to embark on the task of removing any potential distractions, determining task priorities, and enhancing the ability to concentrate. Subsequently, one can direct their attention towards cultivating self-discipline and enhancing overall productivity.

Direct your attention towards what holds true importance in order to effectively attain your objectives through the enhancement of efficiency, the prioritization of tasks with significant worth, and the elimination of activities that waste valuable time.

Evaluate the amount of time you allocate each day to diverting your attention towards social media or engaging in the consumption of videos documenting the lives of others. Consider whether this time is effectively contributing towards the attainment of your individual or vocational aspirations.

So, what measures must one take to achieve success?
1. Cultivate efficacious routines that will pave the way for your achievement. 2. Develop and adopt effective practices that will lead to your success. 3. Establish productivity-enhancing habits that will propel you towards your goals. 4. Build a repertoire of high-performance behaviors that will

facilitate your personal and professional triumph.

2. Eliminate activities that consume valuable time and hinder your ability to meet deadlines, while enhancing focus to achieve double the productivity in half the duration.

3. Eliminate distractions and maintain unwavering focus on essential objectives in order to successfully attain both your personal and professional aspirations.

4. Attain a state of profound concentration and enhance your ability to focus

5. Carry out appropriate actions at the appropriate moment

6. Enhance your efficiency and cultivate cognitive agility to expedite learning, thereby enhancing your professional efficacy and optimizing outcomes.

Time Management

To effectively conquer procrastination, it is imperative that one acquires the ability to efficiently organize and allocate their time. I previously communicated to you my inability to passively engage in watching television during the evening hours. This is attributed to my exceptional ability in elevating time management skills to a completely new standard. I perceive each and every minute as an opportunity for further achievement, and I encourage you to adopt the same perspective.

Have you ever retired to bed in a state of distress due to not having achieved your desired goals throughout the course of a particular day? Have you given consideration to how you could have utilized your time more efficiently had you possessed the requisite abilities? Have you experienced a sense of inadequacy due to being unable to effectively organize your life?

I have also experienced similar sentiments. I have consistently harbored a sense of disappointment regarding my inability to ascertain the appropriate course of action at the appropriate juncture. This led me to believe that attaining success autonomously was an unattainable feat, yet my assumptions proved to be mistaken.

40. To effectively manage your time, it is imperative to initiate the process of regaining control over your mornings. In the past, our grandparents would rise at 4 am to commence their day. Although they retired to bed slightly earlier than our present routine, they comprehended that by seizing their mornings as a sacred time, they could accomplish a greater amount of tasks. Please endeavor to wake up slightly earlier in order to accomplish more daily tasks. Initially, individuals may experience a sense of fatigue and may require an additional serving of coffee, yet one's body will gradually adapt to the circumstances.

Commencing your mornings with a physical workout, proceeding with a cleansing shower, and subsequently indulging in a nourishing breakfast, constitutes an exemplary approach. Upon completion of your meal, you will find gratification in being industrious and accomplishing your objectives.

41. Subsequently, it is imperative to consider the surrounding milieu. There is limited control over one's work environment, however, the desire is to have a home environment that is not only comfortable but also serves as a source of inspiration and motivation. If one chooses to work from home, it is essential to establish a dedicated workspace that fosters optimal productivity. This matter is of great significance. If arranging a calendar above your monitor to keep track of all your assignments aids in fostering a productive working atmosphere, please feel free to make use of any such strategies that are conducive to enhancing your sense of productivity within that space.

42. Set goals each day. As an illustration, if one desires to make a concerted effort towards increasing physical activity and adopting a healthier diet, it is prudent to carefully deliberate on the specific actions one intends to undertake on a daily basis to achieve this objective. It is imperative that you include this in your daily list of objectives. It is imperative to commence each day by outlining a set of objectives to strive for, and to conclude each day by formulating a roster of aspirations for the ensuing day.

43. Simplify your routine. If there are elements present in your life that you can eliminate to streamline your daily routine, it is imperative that you take the necessary steps to do so.

44. Develop triggers. This is very important. If one strives to cultivate a particular behavior, one will invariably establish stimuli that elicit that behavior. For instance, if one were to promptly change into workout attire upon waking up, it would serve to facilitate immediate engagement in exercise. If you neglect the prompt to change into your exercise

attire, you will experience a sense of absence, thereby prompting a reminder to engage in physical activity.

45. Stop multitasking. I frequently receive remarks regarding individuals' exceptional multitasking abilities. My reply to them would be that their approach seems to lack full commitment and dedication, as they consistently seem to only give partial effort in all their endeavors. Please refrain from engaging in such activities, as it appears that you are not exerting your utmost effort in the tasks at hand. This lack of commitment may lead to potentially detrimental errors, depending on the nature of the tasks being performed. Devoting your attention exclusively to a single task not only alleviates stress, but also amplifies productivity within a condensed timeframe.

Strategic Planning Is Crucial: Maintain Comprehensive Lists And Utilize Available Resources

According to a knowledgeable individual, the plan holds little value, but the process of planning is of utmost importance. We each possess ambitious aspirations concerning a particular matter. It offers a valuable opportunity to attain a deeper understanding of your life goals. However, it is imperative that we acknowledge the importance of charting the course of the plan, lest it subside into a mere aesthetic, a vague remnant tucked away in the recesses of our thoughts.

Maintaining comprehensive records is the most effective approach to remain focused and aligned with one's goals. The trajectory towards a specific objective may initially appear straightforward, yet one may find themselves unexpectedly embroiled in a plethora of bureaucratic documentation, supplementary tasks, and inquiries from individuals that necessitate additional time and exertion on one's part. All of these impediments can cause you considerable distress and divert your attention away from your objective.

Start making lists. Not exclusively limited to to-do lists, but encompassing a wide array of list types. Your diary may be categorized as a form of record-keeping practice, as is the grocery list affixed to your refrigerator. You are likely aware of the convenience your diary provides when attempting to recall the timing of your most recent altercation with your friend. To assist you in this regard, we shall present you with an assortment of list formats, allowing you to determine the one that will serve as your invaluable aid:

Shopping lists are an indispensable requirement for every household. It is advisable to make a note of all the items you require as soon as you remove the final item from the refrigerator. Consider incorporating a bulletin board in your kitchen where stickers can be affixed, or alternatively, store them neatly in a stack on the refrigerator itself. Over time, you will acquire knowledge about the items that necessitate weekly purchases versus those that fall under your monthly shopping list. One can create computerized tables to record the weekly purchased products and subsequently append the newly acquired items beneath the existing weekly entries.

Another arduous and time-consuming ordeal we frequently encounter is the task of procuring gifts. Be it Christmas, Mother's Day, Father's Day, or any other occasion. By what authority do we conclude that one cannot make premeditated arrangements for gift-giving? Ensure that you retain your notebook within reach should you encounter something that you believe individuals in your acquaintance might appreciate. You might not recollect all the gift suggestions you have encountered throughout the year, thus, when a significant occasion such as New Year's or a birthday arises, you can easily refer to your notebook and employ it as a compendium for ideas.

Inventory lists - These kinds of lists prove to be useful when there is a need to come adequately prepared for a meeting or event. Under the duress of stress, it is common to experience lapses in memory. Therefore, it is prudent to maintain a comprehensive log of indispensable items required for any given interaction or occasion. Suppose you are tasked with delivering a presentation. Your inventory must encompass all the requisite components for ensuring its success. The aforementioned items may comprise:

- Duplicates of the project's outline • Replicas of the project's outline • Reproductions of the project's outline

- Product prototype • Product demonstration • Product sample • Product mock-up

- Laptop, presentation slides, projector, and other related equipment.

- Additional battery or an auxiliary power cord.

- Writing instruments: available in red, blue, and black options

- Lucky charm

Compilation of Resources - when you come across a reliable and apt source of information, organize and classify it for future reference. In this era, avail yourself of the resources accessible to us, considering we inhabit the contemporary age. One may opt to establish multiple folders within their browser, each bearing distinct titles such as "recipes," "news," "fun," "movies," and so forth, in order to enhance efficiency during critical search instances.

Numerous web browsers offer the function to establish multiple user profiles. One could designate one user profile as "Work" to be used during professional activities, create a separate profile labeled "Home" for leisure browsing, and additionally, one could create distinct user profiles for each member of the household who utilizes the same computer, thereby preventing the merging of browsing history and analytics data.

Opening a dedicated Gmail account for work purposes would yield substantial advantages. In this manner, in the event that your supervisor requires a record of your work activities or requests clarification on the origins of the information, you can conveniently access your account and conduct a search for the sources that were utilized. If you hold a managerial position, kindly request that your subordinates utilize the designated email address provided to ensure efficient monitoring of their professional achievements.

Compilation of Concepts - Our minds generate a plethora of ideas throughout the course of a day, yet often we retain only a small fraction, or occasionally none at all. On numerous occasions, one may come across a scenario that incites them to embark on an alternative path of action. Occasionally, it might be advantageous to examine a particular aspect from an alternative vantage point, or the precise term you were seeking may have spontaneously surfaced while you were engaged in hand hygiene within the lavatory. Record these minor details in a notebook and review the list on a daily basis.

Financial indexes - this can be particularly challenging, especially in the absence of proficient organizational abilities. Maintaining a comprehensive record of your expenditures in a categorized list will provide you with substantiated documentation of the allocation of your finances. In order to accomplish this effectively, it is important to retain the receipts for all purchases made. If you have inadvertently neglected to bring your receipt, kindly record the details of the item either on your smartphone or in a dedicated notation medium. Upon the conclusion of the month, when you engage in the computation of the aggregate amounts, you shall discern the precise sum expended on sustenance, utilities, recreational activities, and government levies. Over time, you will acquire the knowledge of what is essential and what can be omitted. Such lists redirect attention to the broader perspective and provide insights into areas and methods for potential reduction.

Catalogs of objectives - these are the most intricate lists and necessitate particular consideration. It will be necessary for you to individually assess each one and determine the resources and timeframe required to accomplish them. The establishment of an objective and the formulation of a strategic blueprint to attain it, will serve as a catalyst for your motivation and fully leverage your potential. Lacking one, you may risk expending your endeavors and time towards the realization of another individual's aspirations and accomplishments.

Drawing from the concept of the Zeigarnik Effect, it is observed that individuals have a tendency to retain uncompleted tasks in their memory more prominently than those tasks they have already accomplished. For optimum organizational convenience, it is advised to maintain a readily accessible notebook in either your mobile device or handbag, encompassing both completed tasks and pertinent information that may potentially elude your memory in the future. The former option will assist you in effectively monitoring your accomplished objectives. According to the Zeigarnik effect, it is common for us to forget about tasks that have been completed. Therefore, having a record of everything you have accomplished during the day or week can serve as a helpful reminder. Certain days can be incredibly hectic, leaving one uncertain of their cognitive abilities, while simultaneously feeling an inadequate sense of accomplishment. Maintain a comprehensive record of your completed tasks, and you will be astounded by the extent of your productivity.

Numerous tools are at your disposal provided you exert the effort to premeditate. Transitioning from traditional pen-and-paper record keeping to modern mobile applications designed to enhance convenience and efficiency in everyday tasks. There exists a specifically tailored device known as a personal digital assistant or PDA, which facilitates the creation of lists and maintenance of contacts while being mobile. In contemporary times, this concept lacks prevalence due to the enhanced functionality that modern mobile phones possess, rendering it less favored among individuals.

Contemporary applications and virtual assistants offer diverse alternatives nowadays. In the calendar, it is possible to allocate distinct colors to each category of task, facilitating their identification without necessitating the reading of individual entries. For instance, allocate the color red to represent meetings, designate green for events, and assign the color blue to denote the act of making phone calls or sending emails. The application may possess the ability to categorize various tasks based on their priority, category, or date. The majority of these applications provide the feature of sending advance notifications and allow users to specify the exact timing for these reminders. For instance, one can set reminders to be sent at intervals such as 3 hours prior to the deadline, a day before, a week in advance, and so on. Moreover, one noteworthy advantage is that contemporary gadgets are equipped with internet connectivity. Therefore, it is essential to utilize platforms such as Google Drive, Dropbox, and similar services in order to effortlessly store and exchange files, documents, and photographs as per your requirements.

It would be advisable to create various categories of lists and employ multiple forms of assistance. Obtain a digital aide to facilitate your day-to-day agenda and job-related responsibilities. Ensure that you keep a notepad conveniently available within either your purse or pocket to capture any minor thoughts or ideas that may arise throughout the course of the day. Install a notice board adjacent to your refrigerator where you can diligently record and monitor the utilization of consumable items. Utilize the audio recording feature on your mobile device to document the items that are presently not feasible to transcribe. The brief moments dedicated to jotting down notes are not factored into our calculations; nevertheless, upon reflection, you will come to appreciate that this effort has resulted in the preservation of precious time, affording you the opportunity to derive greater enjoyment from life.

"Strategies For Maintaining Singular Focus On Individual Tasks"

By effectively alternating between engaging in phone conversations, browsing the internet, and taking notes, one can maximize productivity within a limited timeframe, correct? Incorrect! In addition to consuming valuable time and hindering efficiency, engaging in multitasking may also diminish the quality of your output.

Forget to multitask. Successfully managing your workload does not involve relying on multitasking. "Place greater emphasis on completing tasks individually and sequentially." According to the researchers of the study, adhering to a sequential completion of tasks leads to more effective time management. Engaging in frequent task transitions does not facilitate optimal time utilization.

Individuals who are preoccupied with numerous responsibilities often face numerous distractions which can pose a significant challenge when it comes to managing and navigating them effectively. Nevertheless, it is not imperative for it to be so. It is feasible to establish job prioritization and identify the areas that demand the utmost attention, subsequently, endeavor to accomplish the most pivotal tasks by effectively minimizing distractions.

Prioritizing Tasks
Please document all of the tasks you need to complete. In cases where one is experiencing a sense of being overwhelmed, fraught with stress, and lacking focus, the act of constructing a comprehensive list emerges as a straightforward and expeditious means of assessing the situation and facilitating a strategic approach. To ascertain the present priorities and determine appropriate strategies for relegating other matters, it is advisable to compile a comprehensive inventory encompassing salient thoughts and concerns.

Immediate tasks should consist of matters that are of utmost importance. What tasks are to be completed today or by the end of the week? It is imperative that you choose the timeframe, while ensuring its immediate nature.

Long-term objectives hold substantial importance as well, provided they are perceived as a culmination of a comprehensive set of actionable short-term measures. If attaining the goal of becoming a doctor is one of your long-term aspirations, one that is causing you significant stress, it is important to recognize that it cannot be accomplished within a short timeframe, such as before dinner. However, you are encouraged to initiate the process of exploring medical colleges.

Order the list

The manner in which you choose to assign a value to the activities and promote them is contingent upon your discretion and the manner in which you choose to present them in your inventory. Nevertheless, there exist numerous approaches to addressing this matter that can greatly facilitate your tasks. Refrain from dedicating an exorbitant amount of time to fine-tuning the list; instead, rely on your intuition and arrange the items in sequence, allowing you to commence promptly. One approach is the implementation of the A, B, C system, which categorizes tasks based on:

A: Critical and highly important tasks that require immediate completion today. Example: Please ensure that the report is completed by today's 4:30pm deadline.

B: An undertaking that may not be of immediate concern, but will ultimately attain a status of high priority. Example: Consolidate all tax documents in preparation for timely filing by the following month.

C: Tasks of lesser significance, albeit requiring completion.

Arrange in accordance with significance
Enumerate the most noteworthy assignments on your agenda and prioritize them by arranging them at the apex, based on the level of importance

these tasks hold for you. Therefore, if you have made the decision to compose a term paper presently, it would be prudent to prioritize tasks such as tidying your laundry and returning a RedBox DVD before proceeding.

Arrange according to level of complexity
Certain individuals may find it advantageous to prioritize the most challenging tasks at the beginning in order to promptly address them, whereas others may favor commencing with smaller tasks and gradually tackling more significant ones. Prioritizing the completion of your math homework ahead of delving into a chapter of your history course could significantly enhance your abilities to concentrate.

Please provide an approximate duration for each task.
Furthermore, it is advantageous to create a succinct estimation of the time required to accomplish each task for every product. Once more, refrain from investing excessive time in calculations or becoming overly preoccupied with this specific detail. You do not

necessitate an actual numerical value; merely classify each item into the respective categories of 'Quick' or 'Slow' for a clearer understanding of when to allocate each task.

In the event that you comprehend that it is highly unlikely for you to accomplish the entirety of your history research within the allotted ten minutes, it would be prudent to set it aside and utilize your time for other activities. Initiate the laundering process, or craft a heartfelt expression of appreciation to an individual with whom you have been intending to establish contact.

Select the initial task on your agenda

Upon careful evaluation of the task's significance, it is imperative that you rank something at the top of the hierarchy. Determine the matter that requires your immediate focus and ensure that you direct your attention towards it. While it may rank as the foremost element in the documentation or even occupy a considerable amount of time, it remains an endeavor that necessitates your dedicated effort and consistent refinement until it reaches a stage of completion that aligns with your objectives.

Put the list off. Rest assured and be assured in the knowledge that you have compiled a task list, which you can set aside and disregard temporarily. Once you have a clear comprehension of the task at hand, it would be counterproductive and impede your focus to have the list continuously looming over you.

Please stow the list in a drawer or an alternate location where it remains out of sight and beyond your access. Presently, the matter of utmost importance pertains solely to the item at the forefront of your agenda.

Desktop stickers serve as highly effective reminders for a significant number of individuals using notebooks, yet it is advisable to discreetly conceal them when requiring focused attention. Do not excessively focus on the upcoming event you need to arrange, especially if you are currently working on a term paper. Position the list atop your cranium by situating it beyond visual range.

Create a comprehensive inventory of circumstances that are presently unattainable.

Despite its contrary nature, eliminating tasks from your cognitive agenda will enable you to allocate your resources towards fulfilling the truly essential responsibilities at hand. For example:

You will be required to extend your working hours. Hence, you are unable to prepare dinner this evening.

The scheduling of your interstate meeting is in direct conflict with the yearbook meeting. It is not feasible to concurrently engage in both activities.

Chapter 4: Establishing Priorities and Creating a Timetable

What is prioritization?

Prioritization encompasses the process of discerning the comparative significance or immediacy of a matter.

What is the rationale behind the need for task prioritization?

When confronted with multiple responsibilities within a specific timeframe, we experience a sense of being overwhelmed as it becomes impractical to tackle them simultaneously. In order to mitigate any potential uncertainty regarding task prioritization and establish a framework for timely accomplishment of all goal-related activities, it is imperative that we determine the hierarchy of tasks based on their significance and pressing nature.

The act of prioritization enables us to establish a logical order, allocate dedicated time to each task, and concentrate on specific tasks while minimizing potential distractions. Through this methodology, we are able to achieve greater efficiency and productivity.

Benefits of Prioritisation:
Significant reductions in stress and anxiety can be expected, if not entirely alleviated.

An excessive amount of work imposes upon us a burdensome predicament, which subsequently gives rise to feelings of stress and anxiety. Nevertheless, by cataloguing all the tasks in accordance with their degree of urgency and significance, we can determine the initial task to undertake, followed by subsequent ones, in sequential fashion. Based on the available options, we have the ability to select and undertake one or two tasks and concentrate solely on one until its completion. Consequently, each task can be satisfactorily completed in sequence. This not only enhances self-assurance but also liberates us from feelings of unease and stressful circumstances.

It enhances our overall productivity.
By directing our attention solely towards a singular task, thereby eliminating all potential sources of distraction, we allocate our energy and efforts optimally, leading to enhanced performance and increased efficiency.

We are afforded additional time to unwind and decompress.

Due to our enhanced productivity, we are able to complete our duties in a shorter duration, allowing us additional leisure moments to unwind and cherish meaningful moments with our loved ones.

Procrastination gets killed.

Given that the tasks have been systematically organized and assigned priority, our apprehension regarding the volume of work has been alleviated. We should concentrate our efforts on a singular objective to swiftly and efficiently address it. The presence of procrastination, which had been impeding our progress, dissipates.
Efficiency has been enhanced.

Given our ability to concentrate solely on one task, we can allocate our complete effort towards executing it efficiently and accurately, resulting in enhanced productivity and reduced mistakes.

How to effectively allocate priorities to the tasks at hand.
Firstly, it is imperative to thoroughly examine the checklist to ensure that no tasks necessary for achieving the predefined objectives have been omitted. If there are any additional items, please include them to ensure that the list is comprehensive.
Please make a notation of the time needed for the completion of each task.
Degree of significance or immediacy.
Deadline for completion

Given the aforementioned information, we ascertain the tasks can be classified into four distinct categories by employing two different methods.
In accordance with the instructions provided in the subsequent explanation of the Eisenhower Matrix.
In accordance with the Pareto Principle,

The Ivy Lee Technique

One of the most effective productivity systems also happens to be one of the most straightforward. The method in question is commonly referred to as The Ivy Lee Method.

At the conclusion of each workday, it is recommended to make a written record of the six utmost essential tasks that should be addressed the following day. Please refrain from exceeding six tasks in your written record.

Please arrange the aforementioned six items based on their genuine significance.

When the next day dawns, direct your entire focus solely towards the initial assignment. Ensure completion of the initial task prior to commencing the subsequent task.

Proceed with the remainder of your list utilizing a similar methodology. Ultimately, transfer any incomplete tasks to a fresh list consisting of six objectives for the subsequent day.

Perform this procedure on a daily basis during business hours.

It eliminates the hindrance associated with initiation. The principal obstacle in completing most tasks is commencing them. Initiating and commencing can present challenges, yet once in motion, the process becomes significantly more manageable. Lee's approach mandates pre-determining your initial undertaking prior to embarking on your workday.

It necessitates the undertaking of a singular task. Modern society loves multi-tasking. The fallacy of multi-tasking lies in the belief that one's productivity is directly correlated with busyness. The converse holds true. The reduction in the number of priorities results in enhanced work outcomes. Upon examining renowned individuals in various domains such as athletes, artists, scientists, teachers, and CEOs, one common attribute consistently emerges: concentration. The reason is simple. One cannot achieve excellence in a single task if their time is consistently divided amongst ten different activities.

Mastery necessitates concentration and perseverance.

Irrespective of the approach adopted, the fundamental principle remains unaltered: prioritize the most significant task every day and rely on the impetus generated by completing it to drive subsequent ones.

Visual Cues

Strategies for Mitigating Chronic Procrastination through Visual Reminders

An alternative method to surmount the predicament of persistent procrastination entails leveraging visual stimuli to initiate your routines and gauge your advancement.

A visual cue refers to a visually perceptible prompt or reminder that stimulates and prompts an individual to initiate a certain course of action. The significance of these factors in conquering procrastination can be elucidated as follows:

Visual stimuli serve as reminders to initiate a specific behavioral response. Frequently, individuals deceive themselves regarding their capacity to recall and execute a novel behavior on a regular basis. I intend to make a conscious effort to adopt a healthier diet. After the initial period, a few days later, the initial enthusiasm wanes and the demands and engagements of everyday life gradually resume their hold. Relying solely on the expectation that you will effortlessly develop a new habit is often a recipe for unfavorable outcomes. This is the reason why a visual stimulus can be highly advantageous or beneficial. Adhering to positive routines becomes significantly more effortless when one's surroundings subtly guide them towards the correct path.

Visual indicators exhibit the advancement of your performance on a specific behavior. Consistency is widely recognized as a pivotal element of achieving success; however, the majority of individuals fail to gauge their level of consistency in practical, day-to-day circumstances. Incorporating a visual indicator, such as a progress-tracking calendar, circumvents this potential drawback as it inherently provides a measuring mechanism. Upon glancing at your calendar, a swift assessment of your progress can be made.

*****

Summary:

Why Do You Procrastinate?
Frequently, individuals tend to generate justifications or rationales to validate their actions. Based on the findings of researchers, there exist fifteen primary factors that individuals attribute to their tendency to delay or postpone tasks.

Being unaware of the necessary actions.
Being unfamiliar with the process
Lacking knowledge in performing a task
Having a limited understanding of a certain procedure Being unaware of the appropriate method
Having no desire to engage in a particular activity.
Displaying indifference towards its completion

Exhibiting indifference towards the timing of task completion.
I am currently lacking the inclination or desire to engage in the task.
Engaging in the practice of procrastinating until the final moments.
Having the conviction that your performance improves when subjected to pressure.
Believing that one can complete the task in the concluding moments.
Having an absence of motivation to commence "
Attributing illness or physical ailment
Anticipating the opportune occasion.
"Postponing a task in order to prioritize and devote attention to another task.
Regrettably, this tendency to delay important tasks can significantly affect various aspects of one's life, encompassing their mental well-being as well as their social, professional, and financial status.
Elevated levels of stress and illness
The augmented demand placed on interpersonal relationships.

Hostility exhibited by acquaintances, relatives, colleagues, and peers.

Strategies for Conquering Procrastination

Thankfully, there exist numerous strategies one can employ to combat procrastination and initiate timely completion of tasks.

Create a checklist: In order to ensure effective management, it is wise to allocate a deadline to each task.

Adopt an incremental approach: Decompose the components of your agenda into bite-sized and practicable actions, thereby mitigating the sense of being overwhelmed by your tasks.

Minimize distractions: Take a moment to evaluate what captures your attention the most—be it social media platforms, news updates, or local news—and subsequently disable or cease engagement with these sources of distraction.

Commend yourself: Upon successfully completing a task within the given timeframe, personally acknowledge your achievement and grant yourself a well-deserved indulgence in an activity that brings you enjoyment.

Block Out Interruptions

Even the slightest interruptions can accumulate and significantly impede the progress of all subsequent tasks. In the present era, characterized by pervasive connectivity, individuals have displayed an increased receptiveness towards disruptions.

It is commonly held that taking proactive measures is more advantageous than seeking remedies afterwards, and what more effective approach exists for avoiding disturbances than completely blocking them? The initial step to take, therefore, is to ascertain that your workspace remains undisturbed and free from any potential interruptions caused by the presence of others. Establish a tangible barrier between oneself and the external environment to foster concentration. Please secure the door, don headphones to enhance focus, and display a "do not disturb" sign.

For many individuals, refraining from engaging in social media poses a considerable challenge. Should you desire, you have the option to allocate a designated period during which you may attend to your emails and online messages, such as during a scheduled break. To assuage any feelings of FOMO (or the apprehension of missing out), it is recommended that you deactivate the wireless internet connection or, at the very least, restrict access to distracting websites.

Skill 11 - Employ Time-Management Instruments

One cannot engage in a conflict without arming oneself; hence, it is imperative to possess the appropriate instruments for the purpose of maximizing productivity. You have already comprehended the significance of utilizing an executive planner; nonetheless, there exist supplementary resources at your disposal for effectively managing your time.

One specific instrument that can be employed is the traditional timer. Every single smart phone is equipped with a timer, therefore it is advisable to utilize this feature on a daily basis. As an example, it can be employed for the purpose of determining the duration it takes for an individual to fully focus on a singular assignment. Typically, individuals can sustain their focus on work for approximately two consecutive hours before necessitating a pause. After determining the length of your threshold, you can proceed to configure the timer for the required duration of concentration. Upon the expiry of the timer, you may avail yourself of a recess, which, incidentally, ought to be regulated by time as well (the standard duration of break-time for the majority of individuals being 15 minutes).

An additional uncomplicated instrument is the timepiece alarm. This particular option is designated for more established responsibilities that need to be undertaken daily, such as rousing oneself in the morning and retiring to bed each evening. Furthermore, intelligent mobile devices offer the capability to set numerous alarms with designated descriptions, enabling you to plan for those predetermined duties. In an ideal scenario, it is advisable to allocate a distinct ring-tone for every task. By associating a specific ring-tone with a particular task, you will undergo a process of conditioning, enabling you to instinctively know what action to take upon hearing it.

There are numerous alternative cost-free applications and resources available for time management purposes. If you believe that acquiring additional discipline, such as adhering to an early morning work schedule, would be beneficial, you might consider investing in specialized resources tailored to cater to your requirements.

Creating A System

The mitigation of procrastination constitutes merely a fraction of effective Time Management. The subsequent course of action entails segmenting your time into distinct portions and allocating productive tasks to each of them that will collectively work towards a shared objective. The issue that many individuals encounter is that they are aware of their obligations, YET they struggle to determine the appropriate time slot for their execution.

Should they commence with washing the dishes or proceed with doing the laundry?

Would it be advisable to commence with your Economics paper or begin by working on the Human Rights reaction paper?

By establishing a system, you effectively establish a hierarchical structure whereby you can discern and prioritize tasks based on their importance and urgency. "Please refer to this informative guide that I have provided:

Established Patterns versus Lack of Consistency

To begin with, it is crucial to distinguish between the established patterns and those that deviate from convention. Routines represent activities that are performed consistently on a daily, weekly, monthly, or periodic basis, encompassing any actions that are recurrent over a specific duration. Exemplary instances include undertaking household chores, completing administrative tasks, filing tax returns, or engaging in physical exercise. It is crucial to discern the routine tasks, as this enables effortless incorporation into your schedule, establishing a regular pattern or sequence of tasks rather than perceiving it as a single task.

Developing Your Personalized Rhythm Regimen

This effectively implies a sequence of activities that you consistently connect as an integral component of your daily regimen. Consider the manner in which individual musical notes are harmoniously arranged to create a composition that achieves an exceptionally pleasing auditory effect when performed collectively. Your Rhythm Routine adheres to the same analogy of establishing rituals performed consistently at the predetermined time and in a particular sequence.

Here's an example:

Upon awakening in the morning, you extend your legs and draw back the curtains to invite the incoming light.

You make the bed.

You prepare coffee while it steeps, and concurrently, you prepare breakfast.

After consuming breakfast, you promptly proceed to cleanse the kitchen sink.

During your time there, it is expected that you will clean and sanitize both the table and the kitchen counters.

You engage in the act of dental hygiene by brushing your teeth.

You are responsible for maintaining the cleanliness of the household.

You engage in personal hygiene by bathing and preparing yourself for professional obligations.

You might be contemplating: this is a task I undertake on a daily basis! Without a doubt, it is highly likely that you have refined the sequence to an unparalleled level of expertise. The task has become exceedingly customary to the point where you likely refrain from making coffee until you have tended to the task of straightening the bed. Alternatively, you might not attend to your oral hygiene until you have meticulously cleaned all the surfaces, including the skin, the countertop, and the kitchen table.

These are all minor customs that constitute a consistent routine – and we often disregard it due to its inherent familiarity. However, what you fail to recognize is that by considering these activities as a collective entity rather than separately, the probability of you omitting any one of them is significantly reduced. If you are habituated to tidying up the house prior to departing for work, rest assured that it will be immaculate prior to your departure.

This is the intended interpretation of the term "Rhythm." If one desires to incorporate a new habit or activity that tends to be postponed or delayed, it is highly probable that undertaking said endeavor within the heart of a consistent routine would greatly increase the likelihood of completing it. As an illustration, you can engage in physical activity during the interval between tidying the bed and preparing a cup of coffee. By incorporating this activity into your routine, it will serve as a motivator for you to complete the task, as failure to do so will hinder your progress to the subsequent stage of the regimen.

Evidently, there are inherent risks associated with this method, beginning with a clear disregard for established protocols. Despite having a firmly established routine, you may still rationalize avoiding exercise and proceed directly to your next scheduled task. This is why…

30 Day Challenge

It is advisable to push yourself by engaging in the disliked activity consistently for a period of 30 consecutive days. Should you omit one, you will need to recommence the count from the beginning. Why 30 days? Research indicates that maintaining a consistent habit for a consecutive duration of 30 days significantly increases the likelihood of that habit becoming entrenched as a permanent behavior.

Logistics

The effectiveness of the Rhythm Routine is significantly enhanced when logistical considerations are incorporated. Fundamentally, this entails arranging a series of actions in a manner that facilitates their execution. An illustration of this could be found in your Rhythm Routine, where breakfast is first organized, followed by making the bed, and then enjoying a cup of coffee, culminating in preparing for work with a relaxing bath.

The rationale behind the Rhythm appears unorthodox, as it unnecessarily complicates matters for oneself. Since you are already in your room, may I suggest prioritizing making your bed before proceeding to prepare breakfast? In essence, it is imperative that a fluid and seamless advancement occurs in your Rhythm, ensuring that the proximity between the initial and subsequent tasks is minimized.

Implementing the X Method

Utilize the calendar to enhance the level of appeal of the 30 day challenge for yourself. Please mark an X on each day that you have successfully maintained your rhythm without any omissions. Please utilize a vibrant red marker to create an X of significant size, ensuring that it occupies the entire box. You may find it astonishing how this seemingly inconspicuous element can significantly influence your level of motivation. Numerous individuals adhere steadfastly to their preferred routine primarily out of a desire to preserve the unbroken succession of conspicuous crimson X symbols on their calendar. Inadvertently, it serves as a powerful visual prompt of a objective, which dissuades any inclination towards ineffective time management through procrastination.

What are the provisions for handling tasks or situations that deviate from the usual or expected?

For tasks that are not part of the usual routine, a distinct approach needs to be adopted. These are fundamentally the tasks that require one-time or intermittent action. They hold significance and at times demand immediate attention, but they do not constitute an integral component of your daily livelihood. An illustrative instance can be observed when one is tasked with composing a scholarly report or reaching completion on administrative documentation within a professional workspace.

Post and Pin

When it comes to tasks that deviate from the norm, a fundamental approach is to utilize the 'posting and pinning' technique. A post-it note and either a corkboard or a blank wall that you frequently observe are the only necessities. Many individuals engage in this practice; however, its efficacy is frequently compromised due to incorrect implementation. For instance, refrain from merely expressing the tasks you are expected to fulfill. Furthermore, remember to include the deadline for completing the task and consider embellishing the bottom of the message with a small emoticon to provide an extra touch of encouragement. For instance, one might consider the task of collecting the laundry on the specific date of November 27th, which happens to fall on a Sunday.

By establishing a specific date, the deadline attains greater tangible significance to an individual. You can now assign a numerical value to it, enabling you to seamlessly incorporate it into your daily itinerary for that specific day.

Arrange by Priorities

When addressing tasks that are not part of regular duties, it is advisable to organize them according to their level of importance. Is it advisable to prioritize studying for your exam before completing the paper, or would it be more prudent to finish the paper before dedicating time to studying? Would it be preferable to begin by cleaning the bathroom or to initiate with the bedroom?

The determination of priority order is heavily contingent upon the required completion timeline and the potential consequences of failing to meet the designated deadline. To provide an illustration, consider the scenario wherein you are required to compose a comprehensive document on Thursday, concurrently necessitating the settlement of your utility bills. Not completing the assignment could potentially result in a failing grade for the course. Nevertheless, should you fail to settle your utility bills, you will be subject to an additional charge in the form of a penalty fee.

It ultimately devolves into a comprehensive evaluation of costs and benefits, enabling the determination of which risks are worthwhile and which are not. Later in this discourse, we will delve into contemporary methodologies that impart skills on how to effectively tackle assignments.

Assign Deadlines

It has been stated that an objective lacking a predetermined timeframe is merely a aspiration, and this principle can be extended to the realm of Time Management. One might argue that setting a concrete deadline for the completion of your Economics paper is imperative, as simply acknowledging the need to finish it is insufficient without taking proactive measures. Hence, it is advisable to quantify your objectives. What is the estimated time required to complete the task? At what point should you commence and conclude? By what date should the paper be completed?

Chapter 2

Planning and Scheduling

Adequate planning and meticulous scheduling significantly contribute to the successful management of time, ultimately resulting in enhanced productivity. By exhibiting prudent foresight in your planning endeavors, you can be assured of dedicating ample time towards execution and successfully attaining objectives.

Effective time management begins with the implementation of a well-devised plan that aligns with your best interests. Upon devising a well-structured strategy, you will gain a more comprehensive understanding of the trajectory of your daily, weekly, or monthly activities. This is significantly advantageous in facilitating the accomplishment of your objectives. Developing a well-structured plan establishes a fundamental framework for your endeavors, affording you greater flexibility to make adjustments as needed. As previously stated in the preceding chapter, an effective time manager possesses the capacity to exhibit flexibility and adaptability as circumstances demand.

Presented herewith are several methodologies for effectively strategizing and organizing tasks.

1. Make a to-do list.

Writing a to-do list is one of the most tried and tested ways to manage your time and plan ahead. Furthermore, the process is highly straightforward: merely document the tasks that must be completed within a designated period and subsequently mark each one as complete. Not only does it serve as a pragmatic planning instrument, but it also proves to be an excellent mechanism for tracking and evaluating your advancements.

There are two options available for organizing your tasks: the conventional approach of jotting down a to-do list using pen and paper, or the modern alternative of utilizing electronic devices such as a computer, smartphone, or tablet. Research findings indicate that the latter has a greater impact on enhancing productivity. It has been determined that the mere process of writing has a stimulating effect on the brain, leading to enhanced memory retention.

One method of compiling a task checklist involves the subdivision of assignments into distinct categories. You can opt for broad, general categories such as "work tasks" and "personal tasks", or choose to break down tasks into more specific types, like "meeting to-dos", "writing tasks", or "kitchen assignments." Regardless of the way you write your to-do list, what's important is that it is works for you and makes your performance more efficient and effective.

Creating a daily agenda at the commencement of each day is consistently deemed advantageous, yet augmenting it with a weekly agenda tends to provide a comprehensive outlook of the upcoming week. It is recommended to undertake this activity early in the week, preferably on a Sunday evening. Merely determine the prominent objectives you must achieve over the course of the week, and designate the specific day in which you intend to complete each task.

2. Simplify tasks.

In the preceding chapter, it has been elucidated that engaging in excessive commitments and maintaining an overly idealistic perspective, rather than a realistic one, can result in suboptimal time management and diminished levels of productivity.

An effective approach to efficient time management and task scheduling involves streamlining and simplifying your activities. Esteemed entrepreneurs who have achieved success through meticulous time management skills agree that it is prudent to "choose your battles judiciously". This can be interpreted as prioritizing tasks and avoiding the temptation to take on too many tasks simultaneously.

An effective strategy for streamlining your tasks involves compiling a comprehensive list of all your obligations, subsequently prioritizing and focusing solely on three to five pivotal tasks at a time. All other tasks will be classified under your category of items to be addressed at a later time.

Leo Babatua, a proponent of minimalism and the author of the renowned book "Focus," proposes that one should address minor, repetitive responsibilities (typically classified as "postpone" items) by allocating a specific block of time to tackle them. The time required is contingent upon the duration it takes to complete the tasks, ranging from 30 minutes to an hour and a half, or more. These minor tasks can be completed during the later part of the day or following the midday meal. Select a period in the day when your productivity is typically lower, and ensure that you have already completed the prioritized tasks on your agenda beforehand.

3. Commence by prioritizing the foremost task.

Babatua strongly advises commencing your work by prioritizing the most critical tasks, commonly referred to as MITs. He emphasizes that one's schedule often becomes occupied and filled, and delaying the completion of the Most Important Tasks (MITs) may lead to their failure to be accomplished during the course of the day.

Furthermore, it would be advantageous for you to capitalize on the morning period when your energy levels are known to be consistently high, thereby enabling you to optimize your productivity during this time. Whether you are in the comfort of your residence or engaged in professional endeavors, commencing your day by achieving your Most Important Tasks (MITs) equips you with the ability to enhance your productivity throughout the entirety of the day. Completing your Most Important Tasks (MITs) on your agenda earlier in the day will enhance your motivation and vitality, thereby fostering increased productivity.

4. Assess the prioritization of tasks based on their significance and time sensitivity.

Significant and pressing are distinct from one another. A task of significance does not necessarily exhibit urgency, and conversely. At times, significant responsibilities are eclipsed by those marked as "pressing."

Dwight D. In accordance with Eisenhower's perspective, it can be observed that matters that demand immediate attention are rarely the ones of utmost significance. In essence, this succinctly encapsulates the essence of effective time management. Frequently, your MITs (most important tasks) do not necessarily coincide with the most pressing ones.

Here's an example. You are earnestly looking forward to a meeting with a prospective client, who indicates their availability for a specific Tuesday. Nonetheless, on that very day, you will have the opportunity to attend your child's parent-teacher meeting at school. Is convening with this potential client truly the most pressing matter of the day, despite its apparent urgency? If your child's parent-teacher meeting at school is of the utmost importance, then adhere to it and proceed to reschedule your meeting with the prospective client, perhaps at a later time on the same day or on an alternate day.

5. Delegate

The practice of assigning responsibilities is primarily suited for individuals who collaborate within a team or oversee a collective of individuals. Whether you hold a managerial position, a leadership role, or are a member of a team within a cooperative work setting, the act of assigning tasks to others provides significant advantages in efficiently managing one's time.

The ability to assign tasks not only alleviates your own workload, but also grants others a sense of empowerment. Rather than consistently engaging in micromanagement and meticulously ensuring the flawless execution of each small detail or task, I suggest adopting a more relaxed approach by delegating assignments to your team members, who are equally capable.

Assigning tasks is a crucial aspect of effective time management, as it affords greater flexibility for undertaking additional tasks and facilitates collaboration and empowerment.

www.ingramcontent.com/pod-product-compliance
Lightning Source LLC
Chambersburg PA
CBHW050240120526
44590CB00016B/2162